THANK YOU NOTES2

THANK YOU NOTES 2

JIMMY FALLON
with THE WRITERS OF LATE NIGHT

GRAND CENTRAL
PUBLISHING
NEW YORK BOSTON

Grand Central Publishing
Hachette Book Group
237 Park Avenue
New York, NY 10017

www.HachetteBookGroup.com
Printed in the United States of America

RRD-C

First Edition: May 2012
10 9 8 7 6 5 4 3 2

Cover and Interior Design by Nick Caruso
Cover Photo by Lloyd Bishop

Grand Central Publishing is a division of Hachette Book Group, Inc.
The Grand Central Publishing name and logo is a trademark of
Hachette Book Group, Inc.

The Hachette Speakers Bureau provides a wide range of authors for
speaking events. To find out more, go to www.hachettespeakersbureau.com
or call (866) 376-6591.

The publisher is not responsible for websites (or their content) that are not
owned by the publisher.

Library of Congress Control Number: 2011920745
ISBN 978-1-4555-1888-3

I'd like to thank the writers who actually wrote these notes, and James Poyser for his musical accompaniment.

David Angelo

Alex Baze

Michael Blieden

Patrick Borelli

Gerard Bradford

Jeremy Bronson

Shannon Coffey

Mike DiCenzo

Janine DiTullio

Ben Dougan

Wayne Federman

Jared Gruszecki

John Haskell

Anthony Jeselnik

Casey Jost

Eric Ledgin

Tim McAuliffe

A.D. Miles

Morgan Murphy

Dan Opsal

Amy Ozols

Bobby Patton

Gavin Purcell

Diallo Riddle

Jon Rineman

Bashir Salahuddin

Justin Shanes

Michael Shoemaker

Jennifer Statsky

Bobby Tisdale

C.J. Toledano

Ali Waller

Thank you, reader, for buying this book.

I really appreciate it. And if you've received this book as a gift, then you should really "thank" the person who bought it for you. Here's an easy way to do it: Just buy another copy of this book, circle the words "Thank You" on the cover, and then hand it back to the person who gave the book to you. If they are a decent person, then they will do the same, and this cycle will repeat until someday when I write a "You're Welcome" book. And that, my friend, is the circle of life. Hakuna Matata. **Jimmy Fallon.**

Thank you

. . . gift cards, for basically saying, "I could have just given you this money, but I wanted to have final say over where you spend it."

Thank you

. . . cones that dogs wear to keep from scratching themselves, for looking like "dog-face martinis."

Thank you

... strange cloud formation in the sky I saw on the way to work yesterday, for reminding me that nature's beauty is all around us ... and that sometimes it looks just like Colonel Sanders' head riding a skateboard.

. . . computer desktop background of a beach that has slowly been obscured by dozens of document icons. Now instead of a tropical paradise, you're like some sort of "island hell" where I'm forced to do work all day.

Thank you

. . . guy standing in front of me in a crowded elevator on the way to work this morning, who I basically spooned with while standing up. If only the elevator was playing some techno instead of Muzak, I would've been all up in that piece.

Thank you

. . . friend who gives me a Christmas CD—on Christmas. Good timing, a-hole. I'm sure I'll play the hell out of it until the next day, when it becomes useless for the next 11 months.

Thank you

. . . office Secret Santa, for making me paranoid. Seriously, WHO ARE YOU? Are you watching me RIGHT NOW? Just hand over the $20 worth of crap you bought me and let's get this over with.

Thank you

. . . tiny children who call spaghetti, "pisketti." Look, just because you're tiny doesn't mean you get to talk like an idiot. Get it together.

Thank you

. . . Good Health Chilean Lime Flavor Avocado Oil Potato Chips. Let's cut the uppity crap. You're a fucking potato chip.

Thank you

. . . adjustable baseball caps with no logo on the front and mesh netting in the back, for being a great way to say, "Hi, I'm over 80 years old."

Thank you

. . . birthday card I'm writing in the car outside a birthday party, for proving that I need to make some changes in my life. Have a great birthday!

Thank you

. . . motion sensor hand towel machine. You never work, so I just end up looking like I'm waving hello to a wall robot.

Motion Activated

Thank you

. . . fat dude with giant headphones on the subway, for looking like what would've happened if Jabba the Hutt mated with Princess Leia.

Thank you

. . . guys in ads for erectile dysfunction medication, for always looking like you're having so much fun. You know, for a bunch of dudes with non-working wieners, you sure are having a great time at that jazz club.

. . . person who buys a round of tequila shots, for basically saying, "I like to throw up with my friends."

Thank you

. . . New York City weather, for skipping fall and already being cold and wintry again. It's like getting to visit Narnia every time I walk through a revolving door.

Thank you

... Christmas decorations, for going up right after Halloween. Nothing says "holidays" like seeing my neighbor replace his plastic Dracula with a plastic Baby Jesus.

Thank you

. . . pleated jean shorts, for being the perfect way to say, "Hi. I look like a tourist even in my own hometown."

Thank you

. . . final boss in the video game I was trying to beat until about 3 a.m. this morning. Everything that sucks about today is your fault.

Thank you

... lucky rabbit's foot. Nothing brings me more karmic luck than clutching the severed foot of an unlucky bunny.

Thank you

. . . the sound of banjos, for making me snap my fingers, for making me tap my toes . . . for making me feel like I'm about to get violated by a toothless hillbilly.

Thank you

. . . red gingham shirts, for making me want to have

a picnic on someone's chest.

Thank you

. . . screen saver that popped up while I thought I was doing work, for reminding me that not only have I made zero progress, but I also haven't made a single keystroke, or even gently nudged my mouse, for the past 15 minutes.

OMELET

EGG TACO

Thank you

... the word "omelet," for being a much more popular way of saying "egg taco."

Thank you

. . . colorful birthday hats, for making people look like gay wizards with really fat heads.

Thank you

... watches, for not being called "clock bracelets," even though that's really what you are.

Thank you

. . . prison, for sometimes sounding extremely relaxing . . . "Wait, you mean I don't have to work, I don't have to cook, and I don't have to deal with my family . . . for 8 to 10 years? AND I get to murder someone? Sign me up!"

Thank you

. . . guy who sneezed in my face and then said, "Don't worry. It's just allergies." I'm always comforted when someone explains why their saliva is on my face.

Thank you

. . . attempted fist bump greeting that—when I realized the other dude wasn't fist bumping at all—turned into an awkward handshake that then turned into some weird mangling of hands, for helping me realize we should just go back to shaking hands.

Thank you

. . . person who doesn't understand sarcasm. No, really, I mean it. Thank you sooooo much.

Thank you

... Fall, for occasionally going by the name "Autumn"—just like my cousin Megan who became a stripper.

Thank you

. . . oven mitts, for making me look like a hockey goalie when I'm pulling casseroles out of the oven.

Thank you

. . . cooking shows, for assuming we all have easy access to freshly ground turmeric.

Thank you

". . . large cold sore on my coworker's lip, for making everything he says sound like, "cold sore, cold sore, cold sore, cold sore . . .""

Thank you

. . . guy refilling his giant one-liter Poland Spring bottle at the water fountain while the rest of us wait. Don't you know? This fountain's for sippin', not preparing for a two-day hike up Mt. Douchebag.

Thank you

. . . dudes who wear berets, for finding a creative and artistic way to say, "I don't want sex."

Thank you

. . . pilgrims, for wearing belts on your hats.

Thank you

. . . kids' table at Thanksgiving dinner, for seeming like a much better time than the adult table. I'm sitting here listening to Uncle Richie ramble on about the midterm elections when I could be over there sticking carrots up my nose and getting big laughs.

Thank you

. . . stuffing, for having the cutest name of any food ever. No offense, pickles.

Thank you

. . . Butterball and Perdue, for being the Yankees / Red Sox of Thanksgiving poultry.

Thank you

. . . aunt who keeps saying that she "loooves dark meat," for making everyone at the table under the age of 35 extremely uncomfortable.

Thank you

. . . boomerang, for . . . ah, it'll come back to me.

Moist and Flaky

Thank you

. . . the phrase "moist and flaky," for being an excellent way to describe a pie, and a terrible way to describe literally anything else.

Thank you

. . . ketchup packets, for containing exactly one-tenth of the amount of ketchup I'm actually gonna need.

Thank you

. . . sound of a Velcro wallet opening, for being the
. . . st sound you hear right before someone says,
. . . an you cover me?"

Thank you

. . . yard sales, for being the perfect way to say to your neighbors, "We think we're important enough to charge money for our garbage."

Thank you

. . . adults who wear backpacks, for letting me know that I don't have to take you seriously.

ELITISM

Thank you

. . . elitism, for being way, way better than every other "ism."

Thank you

. . . fingerless gloves, for providing me with all the warmth of a mitten, and all the stylishness of a Dickensian street urchin.

Thank you

. . . handkerchiefs, for being a classy way of saying, "I'm carrying around two weeks' worth of snot in my pocket."

Thank you

. . . bomb-sniffing dog that approaches me at the airport, for making me panic and think, "Wait, DID I pack a bomb in my crotch?"

Thank you

. . . hangovers, for transforming the sun from a bright happy source of light into a giant a-hole in the sky.

Thank you

. . . desperation. You're all that I have left.

Desperation

Thank you

. . . really small glasses of orange juice at diners. You know what would go great with this giant stack of flapjacks and salty bacon? A $10 thimble full of OJ.

Thank you

. . . pigs in a blanket, for allowing me to eat the equivalent of five hot dogs while I'm at a party.

Thank you

. . . hot chocolate, for being a great way to pretend I'm drinking coffee when I'm actually drinking a candy bar.

Thank you

. . . new study finding that a solid play environment could make babies smarter later in life. Here's another baby-related fact: Babies become smarter later in life *because they're no longer babies.*

NEW STUDY

Thank you

. . . sideburns, for not being called "cheek pubes."

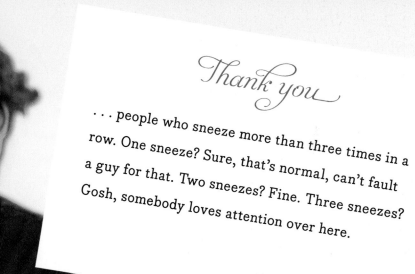

Thank you

. . . people who sneeze more than three times in a row. One sneeze? Sure, that's normal, can't fault a guy for that. Two sneezes? Fine. Three sneezes? Gosh, somebody loves attention over here.

Thank you

. . . lady with a stroller by the subway stairs, for needing help just as I hear my train coming into the station. I know this is probably the choice that determines whether I go to heaven, but here's the thing: I reeeally wanna make that train. Good luck!

Thank you

. . . tiny space between the stove and the kitchen counter, for being an unlucky graveyard for dust bunnies, bottle caps, uncooked spaghetti, and old sponges.

Thank you

. . . red wine, for instantly staining my teeth, lips, and tongue after just one sip. You're like the adult version of Fun Dip.

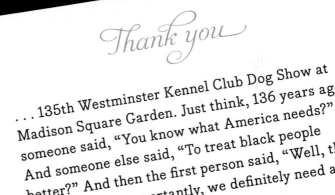

Thank you

. . . 135th Westminster Kennel Club Dog Show at Madison Square Garden. Just think, 136 years ago someone said, "You know what America needs?" And someone else said, "To treat black people better?" And then the first person said, "Well, that too—but more importantly, we definitely need a dog show!"

Thank you

. . . "For Dummies" guides, for identifying the subjects I most want to learn about—and then insulting me.

"Seriously informative with a big dash of humor." *Wolfgang Puck*

Pizza

FOR

DUMMIES

3rd Edi

A Reference for the Rest of Us!

FREE eTips at dummies.com

Thank you

. . . vending machines, for being like slot machines for fat people.

Thank you

. . . lint trap in a dryer, for being like a giant robot belly button.

Thank you

. . . people who clap for the pilot when the plane lands, for basically applauding the fact that you're not dead.

Thank you

. . . friend who says he "doesn't want to take sides," for basically saying you don't want to take *my* side.

Thank you

. . . martini glasses, for being perfectly designed to spill at least one-third of your contents as soon I touch you.

Thank you

. . . guy at the office who says, "Have fun in there!" whenever I enter the bathroom, for making me wonder what exactly *you* do when you go to the bathroom.

Thank you

. . . the Consumer Product Safety Commission, for recalling 169,000 pogo sticks due to potential risk of injury. I don't know if you guys know this, but the only thing that makes pogo sticks fun *is the* potential risk of injury.

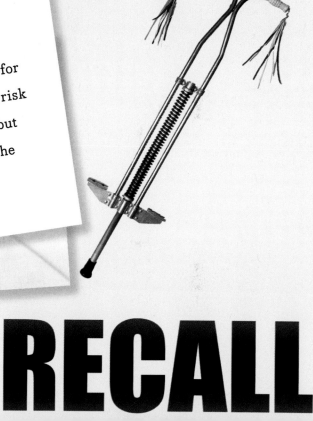

RECALL

. . . gift bags, for saying, "I care enough to put your gift in a slightly fancier bag than the one I bought it in."

Thank you

guy who says he's got some hot gossip but
n stops and says, "No, no, I shouldn't say"—
r giving everyone listening the conversational
quivalent of blue balls.

Thank you

. . . friend who texts me to say happy birthday or congratulations. That doesn't do anything for my rep! Put that shiz on my Facebook wall, where it counts!

. . . romantic scenes in movies where there are hundreds of lit candles. I know I'm supposed to think it's romantic, but all I can actually think is: Man, who has that kind of money in their candle budget?

Thank you

. . . cough drops, for being candy with directions.

Thank you

. . . babies who wear socks that look like sneakers, for kidding yourself if you think you're getting proper arch support.

Thank you

. . . women who walk around with their yoga mats in slings, for looking like either unemployed archers or bazooka smugglers.

Thank you

. . . April showers, for bringing May flowers. But more importantly, for washing away all of March's bullshit.

Thank you

. . . hoods, for being like hats who still live with their parents.

acebook

Search

Ch

Stud

Pr
Pro

Wall

Info

Photos (250)

Notes

Friends

Thank you

. . . people on Facebook whose profile picture is a group photo, for letting us know you felt the need to dilute the impact of your own face.

Thank you

. . . slipping and getting hurt vs. slipping and being OK, for walking a thin line between "sympathy card" and "funniest thing I've ever seen in my life."

THE SEXIEST MAN ALIVE!

Thank you

. . . the term "Sexiest Man Alive," for raising the question: If the word "alive" wasn't there, would someone different have won?

Thank you

. . . quilts, for being blankets made of other tiny blankets.

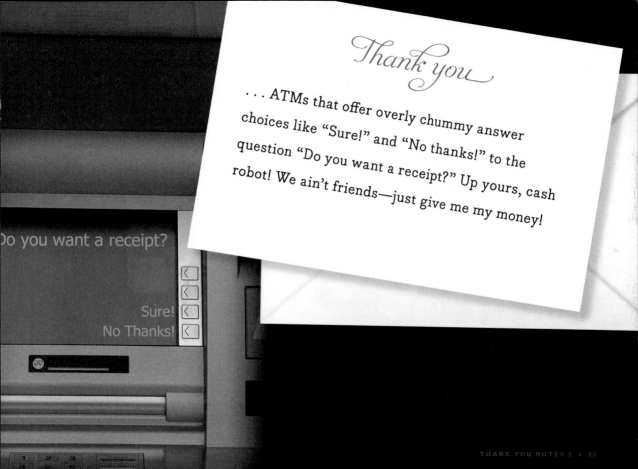

Thank you

. . . ATMs that offer overly chummy answer choices like "Sure!" and "No thanks!" to the question "Do you want a receipt?" Up yours, cash robot! We ain't friends—just give me my money!

Do you want a receipt?

Sure!
No Thanks!

Thank you

. . . bowling, for giving me an excuse to drink while wearing someone else's shoes.

Thank you

. . . rappers who leave the stickers on the brims of your hats, for making me feel a little bit cooler about accidentally leaving that long strip that says "34 x 34" on the leg of my Dockers.

Thank you

... apostrophe, for being a comma that got high.

Thank you

. . . decorative throw pillows, for allowing me to drool on a Monet.

Thank you

. . . rigatoni, for looking like regular pasta that put on corduroys.

Thank you

. . . Mother's Day, for being a great way to tell Mom, "You gave birth to me. You raised me. Everything I am is because of you. Now let me buy you some tulips and a quick brunch and we'll call it even."

Happy
Mother's
Day

Thank you

. . . hard taco shells, for surviving the long journey from factory to supermarket to my plate . . . and then breaking the moment I put something inside you.

Thank you

. . . people who always pick "Truth" when you're playing "Truth or Dare." You should have just asked us to play what you really wanted . . . "Therapy."

Thank you

. . . women who complain when guys leave the toilet seat up, for letting the world know that when you step into the bathroom, you just blindly plop down with no questions asked.

Thank you

. . . smoke detector, for always letting me know when there's a fire—or when I'm making toast.

Thank you

. . . wine opener, for starting off looking like a guy who's like, "Where's the party, man? I'll come!" But ending up looking like a guy who's like, "WOO HOO! I'M WASTED!! AND LOOK AT THE SIZE OF MY CURLY DING-DONG!!"

By authority of the Board of Trustees of the

University of Greenfield

and upon recommendation of the Senate

DR. MICHAEL CRUZ

has been admitted to the Degree of

M.D.

and is entitled to all rights and honors thereto appertaining

Witness the Seal of the University and the signatures of its Officers

Thank you

. . . college diplomas, for being the world's most

expensive frameable receipts.

Thank you

. . . WebMD, for being the fastest and easiest way to transform a simple bruise into a rare, life-threatening disease. ("Oh God, I've got yellow fever!")

Thank you

. . . tassels, for being the best way to tell the world either, "Yes, I'm a college graduate" or "No, you may not see my nipples."

Thank you

. . . the word "unrated" on DVDs, for being a shorter way of saying, "We added three seconds worth of boobs to this."

BEACH BUMZ

UNRATED

"I've got good news and I've got bad news."

Thank you

. . . the phrase "I've got good news and I've got bad news," for basically being another way of saying, "I've got bad news."

Thank you

. . . frozen burrito in the bottom of my freezer, for being the food equivalent of a booty call. I'm drunk and we're totally gonna hook up tonight, but I have a feeling I'll regret it in the morning.

Thank you

. . . skinny jeans, for looking terrible on people who don't have skinny genes.

SKINNY JEANS GENES

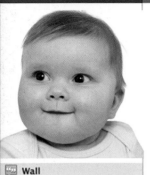

facebook 👥 💬 🌐

Search

Pamela

💼 I.T. Supervisor

📅 Born on January 11, 197
Profile

💬 **Wall**
📷 **Info**
🖼 **Photos** (224)
📄 **Notes**
👥 **Friends**

Share: 📝 **Status**

Thank you

. . . people whose Facebook profile picture is them as a baby, for basically saying, "Here's the last time I wasn't ugly."

Thank you

. . . children who drastically overestimate the available space on homemade cards, for always wishing your parents a "HAAAAAAPPY BIIIIRTH dayMomandDad!"

Thank you

. . . recycling bin at work—or as you're known around the office, "the blue garbage can."

Thank you

. . . dentist appointment I made 6 months in advance, for guaranteeing that in 5 months, 3 weeks, and 6 days, I will be canceling a dentist appointment.

Thank you

. . . jean shorts on guys, for not being called "Daisy Dougs."

Thank you

. . . cheap bottles of wine, or as I like to call you, gifts.

FRANK, GARY, MIKE & FRANK

Thank you

. . . lawyers, for using your last names in the names of your law firms. Because it would be really weird if you used your first names. ("Thank you for calling Frank, Gary, Mike, and Frank. How may I direct your call?")

Thank you

. . . butterflies, for being flamboyant moths.

Thank you

. . . layups, for being slam dunks for white people.

Thank you

. . . dollar sign, for looking like an S that became a stripper.

Thank you

. . . water parks, for being more like giant wedgie factories.

Thank you

. . . hanger bumps on my sweaters, for giving me shoulder nipples.

Thank you

. . . caps-lock, for being the Gilbert Gottfried

of the keyboard.

Thank you

. . . Skechers Shape-ups, for being the perfect shoes for people who somehow care both way too much AND not quite enough about how they look.

Thank you

. . . guy who minimizes his browser window as soon as I walk into the room. Trust me, whatever you were looking at isn't half as embarrassing as what I now *assume* you were looking at.

Thank you

. . . bottle of Frangelico liqueur, for being Mrs. Butterworth's drunk Italian relative.

Thank you

. . . generic female profile picture on Facebook, for making it look like I'm friends with a skinny Darth Vader.

Thank you

. . . guy in the stall next to me whose urine stream is way too strong. Have you been holding it in for three days, or are you just emptying an entire Gatorade squirt bottle into the toilet?

Thank you

. . . stopwatches, for also being 50 percent *start* watches.

Thank you

. . . people who say, "Hey, you know who you look like?" for basically saying, "Hey, you know which celebrity you're a 40 percent less attractive version of?"

Thank you

. . . pamphlets, for being smaller versions of pamphs.

Thank you

. . . quilted toilet paper, for being the North Face jacket of butt wipes.

Thank you

. . . mermaids, for always being so oddly attractive—and a sad reminder that I would probably hook up with a fish if it had boobs.

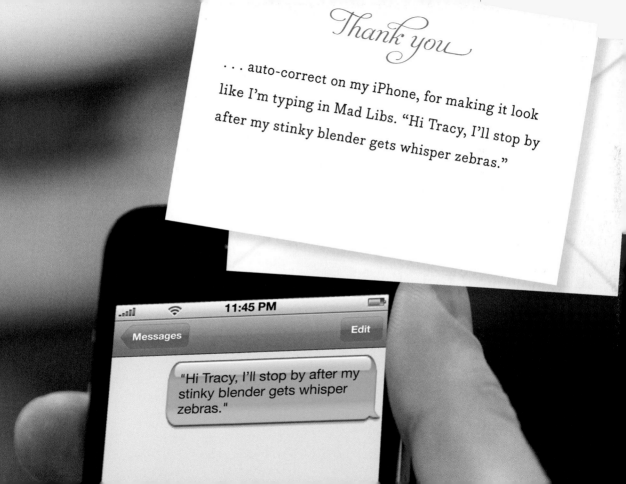

Thank you

. . . Cheerios and SpaghettiOs, for being twin siblings that chose different career paths.

SALMONELLA

Thank you

. . . Salmonella, for being a form of food poisoning, and NOT a Disney movie about a fish who turns into a princess in time for the ball.

Thank you

. . . piñatas, for teaching children that beating the crap out of something with a bat has no reward . . . except for piles and piles of delicious candy.

Thank you

. . . August 12th, for being Middle Child's Day! Not like anyone's gonna notice.

Thank you

. . . computer solitaire, or as I like to call you, "electronic loneliness."

Thank you

. . . Cheetos, for making my fingers look like I just gave Snooki the Vulcan nerve pinch.

Thank you

. . . "just one drink after work," for always turning into "I know a karaoke bar that stays open until 5 a.m.!!!"

Thank you

. . . Labor Day, for being the one day of the year when I'm not the only one getting drunk on a Monday afternoon.

Thank you

. . . Baby Ruth, for never growing up. Cuz it'd be pretty weird if someone asked, "Whatcha eating?" and the answer was "Ruth."

Thank you

. . . new Martin Luther King Jr. Memorial in Washington, D.C., for immortalizing the most influential black figure of our time . . . by making him white.

Welcome Back
Class of 1991

Thank you

. . . high school reunions, or as I like to call you, "Facebook Live."

Thank you

. . . double-decker buses, for showing us what it would look like if buses could have sex.

Thank you

. . . cloudy apple cider. You're like apple juice with cataracts.

facebook.

Share: 📄 **Status** 🖼 **Photo** 🔗 **Link** 📹 **Video** ▤

Happy Birthday!!!|

Thank you

. . . happy birthday wishes, for no longer meaning "I remembered your birthday!" and instead meaning "I was on Facebook today!"

Thank you

. . . denim shirts, for letting jeans know there are other career paths.

Thank you

. . . doggy doors, or as burglars like to call you, "doors."

Thank you

. . . eco-friendly lightbulb, for looking like a regular lightbulb that got a perm.

↰   Archive   Spam   Delete

Don't forget that Dancing With The Stars is on tonight. Have you spoken to your brother lately? Things here are good. Your father's taken up bocce!

● Mom   show details 2:44 PM   ↳ Reply

Thank you

. . . people who put the entire body of an e-mail message in the subject line, for telling me two things: One, that you don't know how to use e-mail. And two, that you are my mother.

Thank you

. . . futons, for being couches that dropped out of college.

Thank you

. . . tanning beds, for looking like human panini-makers.

Thank you

. . . well-behaved wolves. What were you, raised by humans?

Thank you

. . . tambourines, for being the perfect musical instruments for someone who has absolutely no idea how to play a musical instrument.

Thank you

. . . quotation marks, for being apostrophes that are spooning.

Thank you

. . . parents' weekend at college. Or as it's known at college, "Hide the Bong Saturday."

Thank you

. . . any time I've ever struggled to open an umbrella, for reminding me why I've never gone skydiving.

CERTIFICATE OF BIRTH

Thank you

. . . birth certificates, or as I like to call you, "baby receipts."

Thank you

. . . "wet floor" signs, for warning me that if I walk on you, I might start break dancing.

CAUTION

WET FLOOR

"Bitch, please!"

Thank you

. . . the phrase "Bitch, please!", for starting out extremely offensive and then getting surprisingly polite.

Thank you

. . . drinking fountains, or as I like to call you, "face bidets."

Thank you

. . . extra virgin olive oil, for being so pure and untainted . . . unlike extra slut olive oil.

Thank you

. . . nightclubs that turn on all the lights at last call, for instantly undoing all of alcohol's hard work.

BEST DEAL
Only 72¢ an Issue

GUARANTEED LOW PRICE
Save **86% off** the cover price. New York is bigger and
better with new design, new features, more Best Bets.
One-Year — Just $29.97

Name

Address

City

☐ Payment Enclosed

My email address is

Savings based on
U.S. and postage

Subscribe Online!

NO POSTAGE
NECESSARY
IF MAILED
IN THE
UNITED STATES

BUSINESS REPLY MAIL
FIRST-CLASS MAIL   PERMIT NO.   TAMPA, FL

POSTAGE WILL BE PAID BY ADDRESSEE

Thank you

. . . subscription cards that fall out of magazines,
for allowing me to read and litter at the same time.

Thank you

. . . bulletproof vests, for being a great way of telling your arms, "You guys are on your own."

Jimmy Fallon

Type the two words:

Thank you

. . . years of typing on a computer, for making my handwriting look like the security code I have to type in when I'm on Ticketmaster.

Thank you

. . . "original flavor" oatmeal packets in Quaker instant variety packs, for being like the last girl in the bar at 4 a.m. "All the good ones are gone, so I guess I'll take you . . . but I'm not gonna enjoy it."

Thank you

. . . York Peppermint Patties, for answering the question, "How can I make my breath better and get fat at the same time?"

Thank you

. . . Daylight Savings Time, or as I like to call you, "Hangover Appreciation Day."

DAYLIGHT SAVINGS TIME

Photos on pages 1, 4 (computer), 5, 11, 12, 13 (headphones), 18, 23, 27 (prison bars), 28, 29, 32, 35, 44, 45, 48, 49 (fingerless gloves), 50, 53, 59, 64 (Dummies book cover), 65, 66, 74, 76, 88, 96, 101, 102, 103, 105, 110, 113, 117, 119, 121, 124, 127, 133, 136, 137, 145, 150, 155, 159, 161, 162, 163 © NBCUniversal Media, LLC.

Photo on page 2 © MacGregor and Gordon/Photonica/Getty Images

Photos on page 3 © iStockphoto/konradlew (grassy landscape); © iStockphoto/pixonaut (cloud formation)

Photo on page 4 © iStockphoto/Alberto Pomares (palm tree and beach)

Photos on page 6 © iStockphoto/Anatoly Sedelnikov (Christmas bells); © iStockphoto/Olivier Blondeau (CD jewel case)

Photo on page 7 © Jose Luis Pelaez/Iconica/Getty Images

Photo on page 8 © Vanessa Davies/Dorling Kindersley/Getty Images

Photo on page 9 © Good Health Potato Chips is a trademark of Good Health Natural Products; iStockphoto/Thinkstock (potato chips)

Photo on page 10 © iStockphoto/ljpat

Photos on page 13 © Anthony Marsland/Stone+/Getty Images (obese man); © iStockphoto/Nicole K Cioe (subway background)

Photo on page 14 © LWA/Photodisc/Getty Images

Photo on page 15 © Flirt/SuperStock

Photo on page 16 © Radius Images/Corbis

Photo on page 17 © Design Pics/SuperStock

Photo on page 20 © Jupiterimages/Comstock/Getty Images/Thinkstock

Photo on page 21 © iStockphoto/Bronwyn8

Photo on page 22 © STOCK4B/Getty Images

Photo on page 24 © iStockphoto/Elnur Amikishiyev

Photo on page 25 © Martin Diebel/Getty Images

Photo on page 26 © iStockphoto/Stephan Hoerold

Photo on page 27 © Tony Weller/Photodisc/Getty Images (prison cell)

Photo on page 30 © Ryan McVay/Photodisc/Thinkstock

Photo on page 31 © iStockphoto/ooyoo

Photo on page 33 © Creatas/Thinkstock

Photo on page 34 © BananaStock/Thinkstock

Photo on page 36 © Sharon L. Jonz/Stephen Simpson/Workbook Stock/Getty Images

Photo on page 37 © Creatas/Thinkstock (pilgrim); © Neil Beckerman/Taxi/Getty Images (face for pilgrim)

Photo on page 38 © Burke/Triolo Productions/FoodPix/Getty Images

Photo on page 39 © iStockphoto/Jack Puccio (stuffing); © iStockphoto/Thinkstock (pickles)

Photo on page 40 © Zedcor Wholly Owned/PhotoObjects.net/Getty Images/Thinkstock

Photo on page 41 © Michael Cogliantry/Taxi/Getty Images

Photo on page 42 © Hemera/Thinkstock

Photo on page 43 © iStockphoto/Greg Ferguson

Photo on page 46 © Michael Cogliantry/Riser/Getty Images

Photo on page 47 © SOMOS/SuperStock

Photo on page 49 © Jupiterimages/Comstock/Getty Images/Thinkstock (snowy background)

Photo on page 51 © Hemera/Thinkstock (German Shepherd); © iStockphoto/Thinkstock (airport interior)

Photo on page 52 © Exactostock/SuperStock

Photo on page 54 © Jupiterimages/Comstock/Getty Images/Thinkstock

Photo on page 55 © iStockphoto/Thinkstock

Photo on page 56 © Jupiterimages/Brand X Pictures/Getty Images/Thinkstock

Photo on page 57 © iStockphoto/mark wragg

Photo on page 58 © Aubrey Edwards/Comet/Corbis

Photo on page 60 © Creatas/Thinkstock

Photo on page 61 © JOY GLENN/Melanie Acevedo/Botanica/Getty Images

Photo on page 62 © Stockbyte/Thinkstock

Photo on page 63 © iStockphoto/Thinkstock

Photo on page 64 © For Dummies is a copyright and registered trademark of John Wiley & Sons, Inc.; Jupiterimages/Comstock/Getty Images/Thinkstock (pizza)